The Afternoon of The Elephant and Other Poems

Original Spanish Title: LA TARDE DEL ELEFANTE Y OTROS POEMAS
First Spanish edition: Ed. Ala de Cuervo C.A., Caracas, Venezuela, 2006.
Second Spanish edition: Ed. Azafrán y Cinabrio, Guanajuato, México, 2008
Third Spanish Edition: Sentieri Meridiani Edizioni, Foggia, Italy, 2012
Fourth Spanish Edition: Buenos Aires Poetry, Buenos Aires, Argentina, 2014

THE AFTERNOON OF THE ELEPHANT AND OTHER POEMS
First English edition: 2020
© Luis Benítez

Translation by: Beatriz O. Allocati
Reviewed by: George Franklin

© Published by katakana editores 2020

Editor: Omar Villasana
Design: Elisa Orozco

No part of this book may be used or reproduced without the express permission from copyright holders, except in the context of reviews.

Obra editada en el marco del Programa Sur de Apoyo a las Traducciones del Ministerio de Relaciones Exteriores, Comercio Internacional y Culto de la República Argentina

This book was published thanks to a grant by Programa Sur de Apoyo a las Traducciones from the Minister of Foreign Relations, International Commerce and Culture of the Republic of Argentina

ISBN: 978-1-7341850-2-7

KATAKANA EDITORES CORP.
Weston FL 33331
✉ katakanaeditores@gmail.com

Luis Benítez

TRANSLATED FROM THE SPANISH BY Beatriz Olga Allocati
REVIEWED BY George Franklin

THE AFTERNOON OF THE ELEPHANT
AND OTHER POEMS

poetry

katakana
editores

Table of contents

A HERON IN BUENOS AIRES	7
AT THE BATHING RESORT	11
SABRE TEETH	15
BIRTH OF THE TANGO	19
A GENTLE SNAKE	23
THE COTILLION OF DARKNESS	27
THE AFTERNOON OF THE ELEPHANT	31
IN AN ARDUOUS WEDDING ANNIVERSARY	37
LEOPARDS	43
TENDER CRUELTIES	47
A DISTURBING SOUND, THAT WALLS FILTER	51
THE GLOW	55
SPARROWS FROM ELSEWHERE	61
THE LAME ONE	67
TOADS, SINGLE OWNERS OF DUSK	71
HOW EASY TO FORGIVE THOSE WE LOVE	75
ITS LITTLE TIME DETAINED	79
TWO TRACK'S COWBOY	83
TROUT IN THE SOUTHERN SUNSET	89
THE MILKY WAY	95
JOHN CHRISTOPHER'S SKUNK	99
SEEMINGLY	103

THE EXTRAVAGANT TRAVELLER, UP RIVER	107
WHO ARE YOU **TO COME BACK?**	111
ATAVISMS	115
ÁNGEL VARGAS	119
AN INSECT **IN JANUARY**	123
THE QUESTION	127
ABOUT THE AUTHOR	131
ABOUT THE TRANSLATOR	135

A HERON IN BUENOS AIRES

Some brush drew a swift letter S
thin and white
on the chestnut-color water and
suddenly there was the heron,
tourists did not see her
and she did see everything and everyone, swift
and motionless on the miracle of water.
A mirror in the middle of the negligent
city, transparence-painted,
an open buttonhole that clasped instantly all the clothes
dressed by winter.
She stayed still at the fatal bank of her own Amazon,
the disdainful leg folded against her body,
as if to say my balance is made
of a lasting silhouette
and in a lasting way not recognizing at all.
She was a patient harpoon minding only the reckoning
amidst the playful bellowing of domestic ducks,
only she as precise as a minute scythe
in the pleasant Japanese Garden that showed her graces,
with that oriental peacefulness that knows nothing
about the rough murders of a famished heron.
They all went away but anyway I saw nothing:

a second was missed between things, I believed;
an instant in the following instant
was bloodily skipped,
but when the heron flew
another life besides hers was missing in the pond.

AT THE BATHING RESORT

THE AFTERNOON OF THE ELEPHANT AND OTHER POEMS

It took me forty years to reach the Pacific.
During that voyage to the west,
to those waters, like foam choosing
to get to the planet,
I opened doors into weird scenes,
where sometimes someone shouted and other times
the whole theatre remained in silence.
There were hundreds of rooms I crossed
before arriving at the Pacific
I met the panic of living
and the phobia of dying,
two twin brothers.
I savored millions of gestures, grimaces, rictuses.
In the neighborhoods I heard amalgams of laughters,
weepings and whinings, and many more
remained in that foreign heaven
to which one offers his back.
I stand before the site that gave name to blue,
in front of the place where the heavy color
swings between two lands.
I am motionless right at the bank
like the stone a hand throws
so that another hand, invisible, stops it.

Like that going out into the euphoria of the sun
from the complexities of an underground world,
him but a shadow under the extended noon.
Because I'm also that man.
He who, in a landscape of mirrors,
is brought back to his only image
by the waves' reflection,
to live –then and never before–
the instant where everything ends and is over:
it is the jigsaw puzzle being set.
The sun, the scarce grass, the air that is also blue
and the precise stains of the rocks' black
are finally in place.
This is the place where one knows
that raising a handful of the volatile surface
is to scratch the glass of the sandglass.
Where it is understood that these swift
water constructions,
those vertiginous silver ties going up
and soon sunk in the very deep,
are the thinking sea
and that those dark birds –that suddenly soar there–
are its best notions,
those forever leaving.
I am in front of the Pacific
like a man before the fire.

SABRE TEETH

It does not exist but existed and only it knows it still exists:
for its powerful framework of eye teeth and vertebrae
any other detail but the curve
of its huge back happens to be irrelevant.
In its clear conscience watching with yellow eyes
the plain is a single eternity
and man another animal and not the best on
                                            the grasslands.
The tiger's heavy grandfather, it conceals
itself in the step that hides and pretends to be
                                            something else,
the rolling of a bough, a careless scraping
of the wind on the naked surface:
all step by step knows it to be
what imprints those marks
and as regards all, that contact is enough .
Maybe its sturdy stalking
has refined its tactics and arrived
at the height of the waiting on an unknown feline scale.
A patient spring waiting for a million years
for us to cross the mark: our ignorance confirms
that no grace should be granted us.
At a time in several places,

As of yore and always,
(so was believed and is believed by our superstitious
                              notion of things)
is this signal on the floor and also and better
that sturdy shadow that out of itself
builds a hill where the end of our life awaits,
death's pet, certain and brawny.

BIRTH OF THE TANGO

The vertical moon that takes dawn away
and that saw so many things arise and captivate,
the sea condensing in the River Plate,
the street you forgot to name when later,
you added words to the music,
heard you coming out of the blue maybe in a flute
that stopped in amazement, perhaps
in somebody's absent-minded melody.
Of what whisper and beat, of what whistling
                                        without direction,
of what cadence of steps along what spent streets
was tango born, of what silence of lonely men?
The black muzzle and the bitter Creole
that said good-bye to their time
and the poor fair-haired people getting off the ships
and the country in town, with the tenderness
and pain and night and awe
were your cradle and your first steps.
Someone heard the destination of a few chords
lost in the paths of other harmonies
and gathered them turned into the first milonga.

It lulled, wicked *madonna*, in its arms
your youngest tear, tango.
Born of woman, just like men.

A GENTLE SNAKE

THE AFTERNOON OF THE ELEPHANT AND OTHER POEMS

Condescending, gentle enough
to show me its long back,
the deep beauty of its igneous scales
still burning of summer under the April cold.
I had lost myself in my own whirlpools
that surrounded the frozen field
and naïve, as all our silly problems
believed at least to cover the surface
of everything that delivered by us fits
the political division of all creation.
An indifferent gem before my stupid problems,
it cried to me and whispered I am the alpha and
 the omega and also
this simple snake and how much, in effect, I am:
I felt understood in the simple gesture of its rolling tongue.
Between both fields it placed
the absolute curve of its favorite sign,
the avid interrogation that it appeared to be, was:
its skinny body drew a mute question,
and everything that around me consisted
 of the question itself
that the snake's sign enclosed
before the wise god.

THE COTILLION OF DARKNESS

THE AFTERNOON OF THE ELEPHANT AND OTHER POEMS

Broken keys, valueless coins,
those anonymous telephones recovered from a pocket,
the dust on walls, furniture, windows.
Dust covering the whole earth
like a second sea, in dryness.
The stain on clothes continuing onto flesh,
a scream and then a whisper and then silence
barely disguising itself as the rest of the afternoon.
A voiceless call, to awaken looking
for something indefinite bleeding at our side
and vanishing and that we forget by stages.
What threatens us from a fly
furiously screeching on the curtain.
The same situation, the identical words,
repeated every four exact years
with the slow precision
of a lift coming down again.
Things staring at us
from the closed shop-windows,
every time we pass along
with the painful pantomime of ignoring them.
Someone watching us from a faraway building,
exactly when we realize, without hearing,

that he is saying something to us.
The compact horror of the tortoise
taking us back to the Jurassic era.

THE AFTERNOON OF THE ELEPHANT

THE AFTERNOON OF THE ELEPHANT AND OTHER POEMS

To my friend, poet Nicholas Stix,.
wherever he is.

do you remember, nick, the afternoon of the elephant?
you were overwhelmed by the endless rejection
that married woman a mother of four children
had dealt you over the telephone
the only thing she was giving you for
eleven years then
at least
when she was single she said it to your face
and you were irritated really angry
because I had arrived one hour later
and left you alone in huge new york
one more hour to yourself
neither my taxi nor my apologies soothed
your anglo-saxon rage
you said one is alone only in big cities
do you remember, nickie, the afternoon of the elephant?
many rains and snows and footsteps
of italian shoes and sport shoes
passed by that corner in the village

but it hasn't yet forgotten the afternoon of the elephant
you lectured me in your icy english
without realizing that I was also wrecked

and then that huge shadow

you spoke of the tediousness of cities
of the yellow weariness that sets
to the west of your brooklyn bridge
and of the young women crossing alone
and in buses the silky mazes of central park
heading for those rooms where heating fails them

and then those majestic footsteps

you went on saying they had not included you
                                        in that anthology
and said that her husband was bald
lisping and he designed comics
the fool of comics you repeated
the fool of children magazines you repeated
while people
always alert people
ran off the sidewalks
knocked chairs down
and forgot the children in their mad race

you said routine is an old blind lady
begging for coins along bond street and harlem
and that everyone allows her into their houses

then that fat one the bulk
stayed put near our table
in the deserted corner while the cashier
trembling called the police

five thousand kilograms of peaceful forest
crushing the asphalt an immense gray epiphany
four meters high and that funny trunk
with a finger at the end
that tasted fruit from the fallen tables
and hurled the stained tablecloths in amusement

crushed during its escape from some circus or zoo
that old lady beggar who saddens
the oppressed people at home
would look fearlessly at us like all things that
smilingly repeat I am man's friend

IN AN ARDUOUS WEDDING ANNIVERSARY

> *"After the first death there is no other".*
> DYLAN THOMAS

Our generation was a handful of men alone,
a pinch of ruined women,
a cluster of nothingness without shoes,
the bunch of the vines of wrath.
I who agonize
take leave to evoke you though my remembrance
gives you nausea, baby, deep nausea
like the filthy marmalade that those always mistaken
                                           perspire
because they love too much,
though the credo and the miserere we always pray
you and I alone in two nights knowingly detached
by us
—yours, I believe only in me and mine, me entire
                                      and miserable.-
since then they say
that one never never loves too much:
won't it be by chance, in the depth, what no one can see,
the upside down dark Latin of the real?

Everything concentrated frightens at the urgent end
                                    of the century,
it must be finished one way or the other
and this is the mournful gallant of the party,
dressed for the date already
a quarter century begins.
A shame that, in September love,
my September night was neither that one nor this one. A
bleeding spring descends on the self-murderer's night
and nausea inhabits each betrothal since then.
I think I see your dead father with his finger
sinking in the depth where night came to,
your mad mother beating on your face
the indelible monogram of another mad woman
                                      on her offspring.
I think I see some dead people celebrating the wedding,
my right eye -the one that looks into oblivion-
pulls out of precocious oblivion
the smile piercing shame.
My left eye, the one that looks into old age,
a wrinkle of future, a warp of what was soft,
delights in the vespers anticipating
your face and mine amidst the flames
burning like two old photographs.
Was I the ghost of night
and of nights later happy,

the nights and the afternoons
when you bore your children?
Wasn't I the oblivion and the laughter of the spouses,
Mocking at those passing fast in the train,
a face smeared with fury, looking out
the locomotive, the first of those who saw
the mad virgin dancing naked with the idiot?
Give me at least that miserable role in your life,
that one of the wrinkled newspaper moving away
                                      along the road
that goes to a village of cowards
taking the headlines I regret.
Tell me, silent skull today, of what I loved
as far as the very corner of misfortune,
if I, who harbor this fishbowl of images
where even Virgil fits, was not then,
in the laughing darkness, between the lips
of death that in the flowery age
bear all the signs of life,
but the ridiculous and the eternal where what was wept
weeps over what it cannot see of itself, that very self.
Kill me. But not
little by little, like life.
With one word, kill me.
With a single glance.

LEOPARDS

Younger brothers of the huge-limbed lions
and old depredators of our species,
the second-born's of the elastic race
are not made of stains,
but of the plain yellow
where they disguise and hide their certain identity:
it's that they take advantage of the best
nuances of shadows:
is another animal better hidden
than a yellow one under the shower of dots
it pretends? A leopard
is a beast that is always under the rain.
In full noons
they just show shadows
that the extended room of jungles
has left them by habit.
If we see them bicolored
it is just another demonstration of their shrewdness,
appearances are always
the bodily trick of all the little ones.
Neither the haughtiness of the tiger that does not need
our short imagination to be whole
in that word, tiger;

nor the steady and lazy architecture
rising before us showing
the hairy majesty of the savannah;
leopards immigrants to the treetops
are some ethereal and fatal shadows,
the yellow flight
jungles splash themselves with on a well-founded
                                                              whim.
They are the minimum possible for the language
                                                              of death
in its breed of sinews:
they arrive closer than tigers
because they are not what is felt, they are a danger
                                                          with no weight,
the silence, the surprise of a bounce that chooses first,
a velvet-like strategy sliding
deadly and gentle, metaphor and flesh of time
along the thin corridors that link
(and that has always been silent)
the world at peace with the merry nothingness.

TENDER CRUELTIES

THE AFTERNOON OF THE ELEPHANT AND OTHER POEMS

to hunt her as Pygmies do
in the drawing they make of the beloved woman
on sand

they use a very small bow so as not to offend her
and a minute arrow
with true poison
and shoot at her with all their true might
those little ones

those little ones of equatorial Africa
with similar weapons wreck an elephant
likewise knock down the spirit of the she innumerable
(I tell you that this will always be bigger than
                                              an elephant)
reduced to only one
that chosen from the whole

(I want to tell you: from amidst all the whole
and I furthermore add that no drawing has a shadow)

starting from the center
because it's not the poison

no
not even the strength of the arm stretching
                              the dry viper string
it is the living man's power
that the drawing does not understand and thus
                                    it is captured

because drawings do not understand
the frightening power of the small
the minute like the bow and the man
who go out hunting the immense
drawn with colored sand
by himself

remember
because it's always useful

the small
draws and hunts exactly what it wants

A **DISTURBING SOUND**, THAT WALLS FILTER

It's like a purring, yet not a buzzing,
because that precaution is dictated by an old rule,
though stating that the human foe
will not avoid losing the battle on account
                                  of that discovery:
behind the walls millions of invisible ants
go across infinite maps against infinite oblique maps.
They are in every alteration around:
our imprudent prudence serves us
as ignorant wisdom: all that moves
without moving is a carelessness of their stern
        generals.
And under the underneath there is more:
we never understood their parallel world,
that together with ours has prospered
advantageously and upholsters the various deep layers
of the Earth with life.
Ants have their historians
and their poets, singing the victory
foresaid by some faraway prophets,

prior to us and to plants with flowers.
In their world time has a scale
where we are barely another animal
that the anthills see to be born and die.
And underneath, always underneath the earthly bark,
rivers of real continents, not the superficial quarters
we hardly see crossing the garden,
proclaim new republics and new innovations,
uncapable of being imagined, and are hardly
                                                  the possible
to foresee in a sphere that the human mind
stupidly sure of itself
absent-mindedly peeps into its frontiers and believes
                                                                    to control.

And at a different scale than what we call consciousness,
this weak animal that mocks me
that slips from my hand
serves in its own way the power of an empire
that we ignore, his whole life unknown.

THE GLOW

THE AFTERNOON OF THE ELEPHANT AND OTHER POEMS

In one day, he aged two years.
In one week ten.
All of a sudden he regarded his fingers old
grasping a letter that looked,
like him, already ancient,
though its date was that of a newspaper
that hardly, still on the table
consumed the incipient yellow.
On reading it again he made out new meanings
every time:
he was obstinate to find them,
continuously tried to place
patches of favorable interpretations
on the hard, explicit assertion of paper.
The only one.
Then he huddled up on the evidence
still asking for some shelter
and, defeated, later surrendered to the black of the day.
There were malignancies he saw sprouting here
                                           and there:
he distrusted everyone, thought he saw evident
all the bad intentions that, surely,
men keep in their hearts.

The next day
was the very example of the sinister.
He drank deafly in the darkness at noon
and cursed the time and the species
that had engendered both.
Stupid his shoes, stupid the streets,
stupid his address and stupid his surname,
the stupid moon in a foolish blue
on the black and extended ground.
Nothing meant nothing over the world,
where only his letter was.
Then, one day, receiving a phone call,
he had to pretend a quiet voice so as not

                            to betray himself

when hearing reconsiderations, hints,
a hidden entreaty that, very easily and very clearly
he happened to listen to and the promise of

                              sending him

another letter very different from that one
which should have never arrived. He quietly
hung up, considering his universe cleared
and furthermore, the sum of things.
When opening the window, green
had come back to the trees
at its best,
the street glowing as ever,

he listened to the voice of men again,
the barking of a crippled dog cheered him up,
the future was euphoric and the past
saved, even more present
what there was present around him.
Young again by the minute act
of a spirit in eternal remorse
(though he knew it, he didn't care at all,
absolutely) he stretched his hand
and touched The Glow in the air.
It was the only thing he was interested to see
and he didn't care in the least,
the offered knowledge of other worlds.

SPARROWS FROM ELSEWHERE

In what actual place do these little birds
boastful, pluming and heavy
in their minute continent,
from the street prick remnants
of a time that does not finally go away
not only but also thanks to them?

Isn't there in the space they take
like an aura that some see,
where other buildings and even
other landscapes of orchards and woods
in Europe and Asia come to occupy
-invading the minute-
this American certainty
that everything is in its time and place
steadily steadfast,
except for the disturbing sparrows
invading the scenery with other sceneries?

Subtle power of birds
weighing twenty grams
and nevertheless sink under them
the lengths and widths of this era.

Isn't that one in the Paris
that was going to execute Villon
for looting a church
and saw it just like I see it now,
swiftly jump and not fly,
from the ground to a balcony
and from this to a tree planted on that world?

That other casts not a shadow in Iran,
on a courtyard surrounded by lions,
and is it not a king who swings the silks and golds
blurring the ostentation of his march
just to contemplate its grace
exclusively watchful of the breadcrumbs
baked by the Euphrates?

The one next to me
doesn't look at me, but fears
the presence of a child
aiming at it with a sling
whilst from outside the Alhambra
the muezzin of the evening reaches them both.

What do these birds say
about what persists and doesn't leave,
what uses them to state

its continuous miracle and at the same time,
is made only of questions
and returns questions
and in only one question
is contained and expanded?

Little birds that are always retuning
and flying from the unique to eternity,
with your very ignorance,
living, I wish we too were signs
of that of which you are
senses, shapes and that decisive
formidable, architectonic continuity.

THE LAME ONE

So burnt in this world,
like Real Love in just one
song on popular radios.
So hated the slave,
the Negro girl, the dishwasher,
that her masters deflower
every night and she, suspended,
to bloom in a casual syllable,
she, the poor thing, burning -now- only in the shadows.
Naked in the kitchen
after the whiskies, he swears
that there is still only one matter of faith
on Earth.
So helpless in his drunkard's hands
the useless anvil of images
shines ethics, above all ethics,
the lame one.

TOADS, **SINGLE OWNERS OF DUSK**

the greenish trombone in the pool
beseeches who knows what
whether the fertility of its species
always affecting green lust
or the imperative universe that rules us.

hormone sack barely living
between two summers in the filthy water
becoming untouchable: with so much life
death driving the truck wheels
walks along the left side of their throats
and they keep on singing and maybe saying:
I saw the sole of the rotund dinosaurs
at a lesser distance from where it beat like now,
how much can dinosaurs created by man's industry
scare me
how much their cities their stone-throws
or the hatred it has sown over the earth?
The chimpanzee's son like its father
is extinguished early
for sure
and I get its long-winded speeches

green husband of ten thousand eggs
every summer knows that almost nothing remains
thanks to his sister-in-law death
and on which side of that relative
stands your world and that of men

swollen happy instrument
that keeps on turning one after the other
the pages of the eternal score alive
and that doesn't need to hear all the ensemble
to know that its own keeps on filling the room
where for a moment we contemplate the orchestra.

HOW EASY TO FORGIVE THOSE WE LOVE

THE AFTERNOON OF THE ELEPHANT AND OTHER POEMS

How easy to forgive those we love,
on their standard we see the very glory
of our face in oil, hanging from a pardon
in the portrait. How easy the Roman indecision,
the thumb-up with respect to our very costs,
how easy to pay for guilt if our entire treasure chest
is saved from the tribute with its pardon.
Because that anxiety is ours,
the mistake running like mad among the pine-trees
to our very house alerts us and makes us
pay attention to the log burning at our feet, amiable
the temper, extended the hand, attentive the waiting.
If forgiveness be accorded like a sphere,
inclosing all in its gesture,
if one understood to the core
how much of ourselves is hidden there in the foreign,
if the other were subtle, were in the grand manner
to see my hand extended through its tendons...
If it were as it is and doesn't seem,
just as it is easy to forgive those we love,
in the wicked and reprobate the same face
                                        would emerge,
the most feared face, the most hated

would betray the burning depths
of what is equal and the broken boundary of
                              what we love,
the fence trampled by the idiot who is holy,
would be human at the end of the world
and in that manner my surrender is complete.

ITS LITTLE TIME DETAINED

THE AFTERNOON OF THE ELEPHANT AND OTHER POEMS

The car that killed it
went away sure of itself
and now sleeps its motor dream
in a neglected garage in the suburbs

tomorrow they will clean the blood off it
before going to work

the criminal does not sleep though:
he discusses the rent issue with his wife
he has completely forgotten the cat
that until dusk came was made
of sinews and charm
of bloody agility and of silence

now on the faraway street
it is only made of time detained
and is looked for by the ants
always walking
through an endless desert
where water is scarce
but food is abundant
that hidden country where we place our feet

the street keeps on being a street
as it was yesterday as it was
in the evening of death
as it will continue during all
the indefinite tomorrows

the sky hardly darker
hardly someone alone
crossing at the corner
and from time to time another car
seeking some living being

just the cat changed
or its half that is all
that remained on the sidewalk

today when death
has captured another mouse.

TWO TRACKS' COWBOY

> *For when they meet, the tensile air*
> *Like fine steel strains under the weight (...)*
> The Paradigm, ALLEN TATE

it is the horse
the endless flight
the path's nausea
faster than time
the weight of waiting
it's nevertheless faster
there is no man
nor target
for the heavy gun of dawn
returning and returning
gary cooper on the screen
is so thin in it
like anyone else in the world
where his sister of fire
films for 4.5 billion years
the same strand of life
born of a volcano,

from some earthly boilings
and already notes down the ashes sent back...
is nevertheless,
cooper's fiction more fragile
or the strong and formidable gary leaving the tip,
the one who makes a shadow
fitting precisely there, black against
>   the light convertible,
a day in 1952, irrefutable in time
like this woman I see
taking a fruit and that is my mother,
the other hand almost paralyzed
half swallowed by her private twilight,
exactly here?
The two fictions cross her almost always
and all is the crossroads where
doubt returns, dust and mud and lightness too,
is it included, the rope of hours
tying dexterous the Gordian knot,
two paths where one hardly
can walk and walks.
Or are they more and suspicion is certainty,
multiplied certainty,
though denied by the terror
ferociously invading with certainty?

How little spirit, my Lord Governor:
it might be said that an ominous viceroy cancels
                                              his titles,
fades courage, burns all the ships
except one

Nothing, nobody but us,
complains of the mysteries
because they teach nothing, but cast
into a deeper darkness and flee
their palpable demonstration before the eye,
itself a camera too, but for what Eye?

TROUT IN THE SOUTHERN SUNSET

The thread floated loose like a careless man
in the liquid mirror of a cloudy sky

nothing had warned it
in its simple conditions of matter
that a living being had extended it to another
by a cruel unilateral agreement
something that was not really an agreement
between a world agitated
for barely a hundred thousand years of history
(something that looks like an unsuccessful experiment:
every year seems to confirm this fatal
attempt of nature)
and the liquid and elementary universe
that has millions of subtle episodes
congregated in each water drop:
besides refers to the first eras
not to the later
of this great theater 万

the loose thread ending in a hook
in the middle of the prehistoric Patagonia landscape
where the big trout move on

because changeless
everything and they move on
just as in very faraway sunsets
as perennial
as a falling fly

plop!

in the water
a hard mouth emerging from the deep
and advances its armoured jaw towards death
or the life we change into death

does a sudden jump of mind fit
a bright insight emerging from waters
something warning that life itself
is at one end and another of the loose thread
in danger because of the following act
one just like the other in danger
always in danger by a determination
based on habit?

the same dangerous habit
of man and of trout

and then that picking up the thread

and breaking the rod on the knees
throwing the reel away
the decoys the boots
return to the cabin with nothing
with nothing for good of those precious innocent lives
with nothing of that wide liquid universe
forever safe
at least from one of us

And the cabin keeper
watching my behaviour from afar
judged me an idiot

THE MILKY WAY

THE AFTERNOON OF THE ELEPHANT AND OTHER POEMS

salt river in the orange blossom night
of the invisible tree whose fruit
are the worlds of the matter route
to nothing in the star nigh
foam of another wider mire
the reservation of the white mourns even more
the dull door
on a cut of its night there is no wonder:
you the spittle of the devil that takes us
to wander about the garden in darkness
you know that new house
where we are slowly going to ponder
there night raises another night
where you will be a place within a place.

JOHN **CHRISTOPHER'S SKUNK**

I was a child when his road crossed mine
and used to stubbornly take as a prisoner
-always held with a dog leash-
that beautiful black and white animal
to which he naturally gave a ridiculous name
and smilingly said that his father
(a shameless veterinarian)
had removed "the poison glands" from it

john christopher's skunk
that amputated beast
in its convict costume
nibbled the roses of all gardens
as if it envied their perfume
and smelled everything it found
maybe seeking its own
definite stench lost forever

it was hated by everyone
as its sharp paws destroyed the flower beds
and turned over the bricks placed on purpose
for walking across the unpaved streets
when rain flooded the village paths

that alone and the disadvantage of being a skunk
are enough to congregate the crowd's hatred

we all were once john christopher's skunk
an unarmed hair ball deprived of all weapons

a farmer killed it with a shotgun
one afternoon when its god the child
was asleep: he woke up in a dream
where the little animal no longer existed
and saw me and cried
not because of the helpless animal
but because of what his childhood had lost

the young of another animal stronger
than a helpless skunk
blamed it without knowing
for that harm
legs upside down by a fence
were swarmed with flies

a definite meanness walks amidst things ⌗

SEEMINGLY

Seemingly, nothing affects
the slow caravan of days.
Its slow leak doesn't drill
doesn't wreck, doesn't transfigure the hand,
doesn't move away with its ghost
the wavy smile of hair.
Seemingly nothing will dwindle down,
no one will be replaced from his shoes
or from his schedules, nothing will be restored.
All those faces that memory
contains will not be modified
nothing will alter its measured imitation
the one usurping the place of what is gone
seemingly won't be touched.
Then, for what, under the appearance,
like a child feeling another presence
in the room where he should sleep
alone and untroubled at midnight,
we feel that ghostly hand
going around so near, always?
Then, when a door that should remain
shut opens,
why don't we wish to look inside,

wrapped, seemingly hidden?
Scared soul, that envies
the blind, the one who doesn't hear,
and anyone unable
to understand or walk. 🕆

THE EXTRAVAGANT TRAVELLER, UP RIVER

Then I saw it in the oily water,
the gift of the industry and of hatred for the living,
sailing the course up river:
the impossible salmon,
a brawny monster
adorned by greens and violets,
by oranges and reds,
in the livery that only desire lends
to the eager to reproduce it at all costs.
Weird iridescence amidst the trash
of the condemned river,
like a man obstinate
in finding the path saying
"I am your life", a gift
for naiveté obstinate to believe,
a sting for the tightened sinews
under the harsh scales,
an overdose of hormones
flooding the minute brain.
And that mouth open to the desire of breathing
still some more of its last day,
kept the last syllable
of those who don't allow to be defeated

nor even by their own silliness
nor by the edges of the docks
where they never stop, where never
for any one thing they stop.

WHO ARE YOU **TO COME BACK?**

Who are you to come back, with the care of what
                                        is dead,
the gay smile under the worm, who are you
                                        to come back, cheeky,
flooding the green grass where I've just been
                                        buried, burning?
Wasn't I what is dead, didn't your charms prostituted
                                        in the living
finally kill me, wasn't I what was dead, respectable
under a rotten moon? I was safe in a good-bye
and you returned giving me back that suited.
It seems that for your beauty, a moon in its pool,
time is a chimera, what we'll all be,
a slavering time, hardly, without the transparency
                                        of its sense.
There is a sickening abuse in your persistence.
I know: in the pleasant the illusion swings
of something crossing the minute's bridge.
Then you crowd at once taking advantage of desire.
Confused is apparently your way.
I know your horror hides another one further sunk
                                        in the deep.

The three times possible thing persuaded falls asleep:
you have that which is never in the illusion
                              of your appearance;
the triple that names it and that is, at the same time,
                                        the first
bite on the tail of the whole where you exist.
                            Damned light is seeing you.
He who seeks in he shadows of imagination
harmonizes with him who searches among books.
In you it is understood that nothing is worth the will,
                                firmness, one's own.
A manner there is of walking amidst the ways,
and that is yours. Making up another will always be
                                    on this side,
craving to grow in the like that eager of the royal
                                          manner
doesn't touch it, when reached.

Obstinate whim to be the thing in the instant
and that which was, proud, an instant ago.

ATAVISMS

THE AFTERNOON OF THE ELEPHANT AND OTHER POEMS

> *Old houses were scaffolding once*
> *and workmen whistling*
> THOMAS E. HULME

Like an old hallucination
which we are accustomed to:
its repeated invasion,
its excesses, its routine almost
being a piece of furniture, a television program
that the screen has returned for years.
Like a relative who keeps on phoning.
Like a salesman insisting with the bell,
a former girlfriend sending letters and letters
a penalty of time, an inevitable word,
a cliché, the usual refrain of thought;
like a pavane we repeat without remembering
                                          its composer,
its title, the moment when we heard it for the first time.

So this inexplicable certainty comes back
time and time again,
this secret we hide from everyone
and from ourselves

-when we can, certainly-
and when we cannot we see it in its huge length,
its disturbing symmetry,
its liquid horizons, its abysses, its caverns
its familiar roads reaching to our core,
there where someone bows his head,
admitting it, but not resigned to it, yet,

See the shadow of the beast we are
in every act and in every day
guilty and innocent and the third.

We are the building that fears
the tremors that support its foundations,
because the ancient shadow that looks like us
still moves at his ease through the half-light
and the passages of its cellar that lead to the rooms
and opens, from time to time, the parlor where
                                                   we lunch
with so many polite and smiling guests.

It's him, they point, and they stare at us
where we are, at the head of the table,
and also at the threshold of the half-open door.

ÁNGEL VARGAS

THE AFTERNOON OF THE ELEPHANT AND OTHER POEMS

From a gray mist the medium voice
Emerges and the greatest seem
To fall back, like burnt paper
Before the fire of that common noise.
From that so ordinary and his own.
Ángel Vargas, you and God,
Who doesn't exist, know
How much fits in what is vulgar
And that it is so certain like
Folding a napkin in the hand
After eating, at a time,
A bite and a remembrance.
You, Ángel Vargas, maybe the best
On a scale that recognizes other merits,
like the intimate, the dead,
The lost, the ephemeral, the sincere,
The lost again, the most loved,
The most, that is always broken-down
And that is not the fatal,
But the brief glory of its anticipation.

AN INSECT IN JANUARY

minimal at the window, an active presence
hardly different from the air in his elementary design

plus six legs and two wings the green body
just a line crossing
millions of years in his fluttering
from the dinosaurs' nostrils
to the stern, cold present at my window

he was never bigger and never abundant:
when plants that are herbs today
reached heights and curved colossal shapes
a few like him rose
towards the faraway treetops with no little effort
of those same delicate membranes
that hardly move or rest before me

there where he reflects the other whole wide world
which is also his

his victory made of a safe silence
just like all things

THE QUESTION

And is twilight breaking out in red gold,
immutable, beyond the history
of Eastern and Western poetry,
the red golden twilight,
unreachable, the red of a broken star
fractured against the edge of the world,
that which is the first and only one I see?
When, authentic and whole,
here, even though it's almost turned to night,
here, in these verses I require it.

ABOUT THE AUTHOR

Luis Benítez was born in Buenos Aires on the 10th of November 1956. He is a member of the Academia Iberoamericana de Poesía, New York Chapter, USA, with its seat at the Columbia University; of the International Society of Writers (USA), of the World Poets Society (Greece) and of the Advisory Board of Poetry Press (India). He has received the title of Compagnon de la Poèsie de la Association La Porte des Poètes, with a seat at the Université de La Sorbonne, Paris, France. He is a member of the Sociedad de Escritoras y Escritores de Argentina (SEA), the Asociación de Poetas Argentinos (APOA) and the Argentinian PEN Club. His 36 books of poetry, essays and narratives have been published in Argentina, Chile, France, Italy, Mexico, Romania, Spain, Sweden, Venezuela, United Kingdom, United States of America and Uruguay.

Since the '90 several magazines published his poems: *Agenda Poetry, Current Accounts, Dream Catcher, Erbacce, Littoral, Markings, Poetic Licence, Poetry Monthly, The Eil-*

don Tree, The Journal, The Misread Issue, The Text, Urthona, Wasafiri (United Kingdom); *A Different Drummer, Albatross, And Then, Barnwood, Beatlick News, Flint Hills Review, Green Mountains, Illuminations, La Nuez, Meridian Anthology of Contemporary Poetry, Mobius, Nagari, Nexus, Pacific Coast Journal, Poesy, Porcupine, Runes, Sinalefa, Tamarind, Weber Studies* (USA); *Challenger, Existere* (Canada); *Upstairs at Duroc, La Porte des Poétes* (France); *Het Oog van de Roos* (Belgium); *Isola Nigra, L´Ortiga* (Italy); *Poetry Salzburg Review* (Austria), *Kafla, Krytia* (India) and others.

Awards received

First International Award of Poetry La Porte des Poètes (Paris, 1991).

Mención de Honor del Concurso Municipal de Literatura (Poetry, Buenos Aires, 1991).

Premio Bienal de la Poesía Argentina (Buenos Aires, 1992).

First Award Joven Literatura (Poetry) of the Fundación Amalia Lacroze de Fortabat (Buenos Aires, 1996).

First Award in the Concurso Internacional de Ficción (Montevideo, Uruguay, 1996).

First Award in Premio Tuscolorum di Poesìa (Sicilia, Italy, 1996).
First Award in Premio de Novela Letras de Oro (Buenos Aires, 2003).
Accesit 10ème. Concours International de Poèsie (Paris, 2003).
First Award in Premio Internacional para Obra Publicada "Macedonio Palomino" (Mexico, 2007).

Works on the author

Sobre las poesías de Luis Benítez, by Carlos Elliff (essay, Editorial Metáfora, Buenos Aires, 1991).
Conversaciones con el poeta Luis Benítez, by Alejandro Elissagaray and Pamela Nader (Volume I, 1995, Volume II, 1997, Editorial Nueva Generación, Buenos Aires).
Itinerarios: Antología (selection and preliminary essay by Alejandro Elissagaray, 2001, Editorial Nueva Generación, Buenos Aires).
Luis Benítez: Breve Antología Poética (selection and preliminary essay by Elizabeth Auster, 2008, Editorial Juglaría, Rosario, Province of Santa Fe, Argentina).
La poesía es como el aroma. Poética de Luis Benítez, by Camilo Fernández Cozman, Ph.D. (essay, Ed. Nueva Generación, Buenos Aires, 2009).

La novelística de Luis Benítez. Aproximaciones críticas a la historiografía, la mitología y la masculinidad patriarcal, by Assen Kokalov, Ph.D. (essay, Ed. Nueva Generación, Buenos Aires, 2015).

ABOUT THE TRANSLATOR

Beatriz Olga Allocati. Born in Buenos Aires, Argentine Republic. A poet herself she has published eight poetry books as well as other two in prose (biography of her father and a Guide for Genealogial Research), having also participated in anthologies in Argentina, Uruguay, Venezuela, Austria and India.

With still two works unpublished, she has been lately entrusted the translation of poems and books by several poets.

A member of the Sociedad Argentina de Escritores (SADE), she is also the present Secretary of the Asociación de Poetas Argentinos (APOA) and an Honorary Consultant to the Museo Histórico de La Boca, Buenos Aires.

www.ingramcontent.com/pod-product-compliance
Lightning Source LLC
Chambersburg PA
CBHW051653040426
42446CB00009B/1122